CATS of the WILD \ Felinos salvajes

LYNXES
LINCES

Henry Randall

PowerKiDS press™

New York

Traducción al español:
Eduardo Alamán

Published in 2011 by The Rosen Publishing Group, Inc.
29 East 21st Street, New York, NY 10010

First Edition

Editor: Joanne Randolph
Book Design: Ashley Burrell

Traducción al español: Eduardo Alamán

Photo Credits: Cover © www.iStockphoto.com/Eduard Kyslynskyy; pp. 5, 15 iStockphoto/Thinkstock; pp. 6, 24 (left) © S. Meyers/age fotostock; pp. 9, 24 (right) © Christian Heinrich/age fotostock; pp. 10–11, 21 Shutterstock.com; p. 12 Gerry Ellis/Getty Images; pp. 16–17, 24 (center right) © www.iStockphoto.com/Albert Mendelewski; pp. 18, 22, 24 (center left) Jupiterimages/Photos.com/Thinkstock.

Library of Congress Cataloging-in-Publication Data

Randall, Henry, 1972-
[Lynxes. Spanish & English]
Lynxes = Linces / by Henry Randall. — 1st ed.
    p. cm. — (Cats of the wild = Felinos salvajes)
Includes index.
ISBN 978-1-4488-3129-6 (library binding)
1. Lynx—Juvenile literature. I. Title. II. Title: Linces.
QL737.C23R3618 2011
599.75'3—dc22

                                    2010025812

Manufactured in the United States of America

CPSIA Compliance Information: Batch #WW11PK: For Further Information contact Rosen Publishing, New York, New York at 1-800-237-9932

Web Sites: Due to the changing nature of Internet links, PowerKids Press has developed an online list of Web sites related to the subject of this book. This site is updated regularly. Please use this link to access the list:
www.powerkidslinks.com/cotw/lynxes/

Contents/Contenido

Lynxes are wild cats that live in forests around the world. These cats are great climbers.

Los linces son gatos salvajes que viven en los bosques de todo el mundo. Los linces son grandes trepadores.

Lynxes have **fur** that keeps them warm in cold weather. Do you see the spots on these lynxes' fur?

Los linces tienen **pelaje** que los ayuda a mantenerse calientes en el frío. ¿Puedes ver las manchas en el pelaje de estos linces?

Lynxes are known for the black **tufts** of fur on the tips of their ears. These hairs help them hear.

Los linces son conocidos por tener un **mechón** de pelaje en la punta de sus orejas. El mechón les ayuda a oír mejor.

8

Lynxes rest in the forest during the day. They come out to find food when it gets dark.

Los linces descansan en el bosque durante el día. Al oscurecer, salen a buscar comida.

Lynxes can climb to high places to look for food. Lynxes eat mostly hares or rabbits.

Los linces pueden trepar para buscar comida. Los linces comen principalmente liebres o conejos.

13

The lynx's eyes are some of its best tools. It counts on its eyesight for hunting animals.

La vista de los linces es una de sus mejores herramientas. Los linces usan su vista para cazar animales.

The lynx does not have a long **tail**, as some other cats do.

___

A diferencia de otros felinos, los linces no tienen una **cola** larga.

17

Lynx **kittens** are born in the spring. They stay with their mother for about one year.

Los **cachorros** de lince nacen en la primavera. Los cachorros se quedan con sus mamás durante un año.

This lynx waits quietly in the grass for its dinner. When an animal gets close, the lynx jumps on it.

Este lince espera en silencio por su víctima. Cuando un animal se acerca, el lince salta sobre él.

20

Lynxes can jump, run, and climb. What else do you want to know about them?

Los linces pueden saltar, correr y trepar. ¿Qué mas quieres saber de estos felinos?

23

Words to Know/
Palabras que debes saber

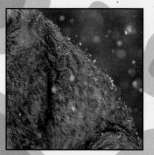   

| fur | kittens | tail | tufts |
| (el) pelaje | (los) cachorros | (la) cola | (los) mechones |

Index

Índice